HEAD
★ V ★
HEART

new & selected poems

HEAD ★ V ★ HEART

new & selected poems
Rob Sturma

MOON TIDE PRESS

~ 2021 ~

Head ★V★ Heart: New & Selected Poems
© Copyright 2021 Rob Sturma
All rights reserved. No part of this book may be used or reproduced in any manner whatsoever without written permission from either the author or the publisher, except in the case of credited epigraphs or brief quotations embedded in articles or reviews.

Editor-in-chief
Eric Morago

Editor Emeritus
Michael Miller

Marketing Director
Dania Alkhouli

Marketing Assistant
Ellen Webre

Proofreader
Jim Hoggat

Front cover art
Gustavo Hernandez

Book design
Michael Wada

Moon Tide logo design
Abraham Gomez

Head v Heart: New & Selected Poems
is published by Moon Tide Press

Moon Tide Press
6709 Washington Ave. #9297, Whittier, CA 90608
www.moontidepress.com

FIRST EDITION

Printed in the United States of America

ISBN # 978-1-7350378-5-1

Contents

Foreword by Eric Morago   7

The Day Before Rock and Roll AKA The Pat Boone Special AKA White Devil Music	10
The Midnight Hour + The Art of Waiting	12
1984	14
1996 Was a Great Year in Music; Relationships, Not So Much	16
romeo & juliet are together in eternity	18
The Last Three Viewings	20
Ghazal Amour	23
Depress Play AKA Wear Your #$&*% Mask	24
Warning Signs, or Dissecting the Spotify Playlist Post Break-Up	25
You'll Accomp'ny Me (after Bob Seger)	26
Night Moves (after Bob Seger)	27
When You Are Filling Out Job Applications by Hand	29
Cooking for One	31
Andre The Giant is Alive and Well and Working at the Circle K on 39th and Penn	33
Plancha	35
Worse Than My Bite	36
If You Missed the House Concert	38
The First Attempt: 11/1/11	40
Dear Poet More Successful Than I Am,	42
I Love How You Love	44
Sailor to Mermaid, or Message No Longer in The Bottle	45
Popeye The Sailor Ruminates on Love	48
Unsexy Beast: A Monstertown Personal Ad	49
Oh, Hey There, Sunshine Gnomes!	50
Bedtime Story	52
Sharp	53
Skyrim Keeps Me Honest	54
Stop Me if You've Heard This	56
What do you get for someone who:	57
Band Geek	58
WWE Manager Paul Heyman and I Go to Hot Topic Because It's BOGO T-Shirt Weekend	59
Poor Thing	61
Lego Hulk Teaches Me About Life on the Last Day of 2014 via the Lego Marvel Videogame	62

Moon Takes a Lover	63
Dry Dock (4/4/14)	64
Pep Talk	66
Tinder	68
All Hail the New Ambassador of Awesome	70
Color the Night Sky	72
You Got Me All Giddy/Up	73
Who's Going to Drive You Home	74
TMNT, or When Did Turtle Power Become So Relatable	76
FSTB!	77
Blockhead	78
Comic Book Me	80
Scream On	82
Gardener	83
Todd Packer Is Committed to Being a Trash Human	85
not a robot / not a girl	87
What I Said to the Mirror	89
This Was Supposed to Be a Buffy Poem	90
Oh My Stars	92
Ghost at an Open Mic	94
Now That I Have Your Attention	95
Lay Me Down	97
Tuesday Night at the Sober Bar	100
Benediction for the Church of Common Sense	102
About the Author	*104*
Acknowledgements	*105*

Foreword

I don't usually have any trouble writing about another poets' work, but—truth be told—this introduction has been one the most difficult things I have had to write.

It's not because Rob Sturma isn't one of the most talented wordsmiths I know (he is) or doesn't captivate a crowd when he performs his poems (he does). And it's certainly not because I don't love him like a brother and a whole parade of other sentimental cliches. So, for weeks now, I've been asking myself why this particular foreword has been so damn hard to write, and I think I've finally figured it out: Rob Sturma is my hero, in both poetry and life, and I don't want to let him down.

Rob was one of the first poets I ever met, became a fast fan of, and then quickly a friend. I'm sure he knows that for the past fifteen years he has been there for me as I've grown into the writer and publisher I am today. However, I don't think he's aware that this whole time he has been a man whom I have aspired to. Now *that* said, it is important for you—the reader—to know I'm not publishing *Head v Heart* out of some debt of gratitude or any sense of obligation; I'm publishing these poems because they deserve to be in your wanting hands.

You *need* these poems. They are a roadmap to parts of yourself you didn't know you lost and a star chart to course a better future by. They weave in and out a narrative of self-healing and survival that is a necessary part of the human condition, while brilliantly using pop culture and nostalgia to reflect on these themes in a way that is unique to Rob's voice.

Rob is both a champion of and master at exploring the world through a lens of all things geek. His belief: that our favorite superheroes, wrestling icons, and video games, all metaphor themselves into the body and can then be mined for poems that are achingly authentic. In this collection, Rob stumbles upon Andre the Giant working at Circle K, gets some solid life advice from his Lego Hulk avatar, and writes a poem that is "supposed" to be about Willow from *Buffy the Vampire Slayer* (but ends up being about so *much* more); not a single one of these ideas could have been birthed by a different poet, nor their execution matched.

Now you may be thinking how does a poet who uses pop culture the way Rob does write anything of nuance and complexity?

That's where you'd be surprised—the answer is quite easily. Popular culture is a scalpel in Rob's steady hands and with it he can cut into our hearts and show us how its messy insides work. Don't be fooled by the accessible—sometimes silly—subject matter of his poems; they are anything but simple. That is the cleverness of his craft. Rob can write about Lego Hulk smashing bricks, suckering us in with a funny title and premise, only to then land a gut-punch nugget of truth only a poem about Lego Hulk can: "Everything looks impossible, but really, everything is just made of bricks. Bricks can be smashed." The poem concludes by informing the reader: "You are so necessary." I believe that is this collection's battle cry—its call to arms. Rob's poems are an army of hugs.

But Rob doesn't just write poems to lift the reader out from the dark—he is so courageously pulling the darkness out of himself. Each poem is a piece of his own recovery. I am in awe of how he has been able to battle his demons—write about them—with the all the flair and bravery of an 80's *WrestleMania* Heavyweight Champion walking into the ring for a fight that's still being scripted, body slam after body slam.

That is what a hero does.

So, no, publishing Rob Sturma is the furthest thing from obligation. It's an honor. Now, brace yourself for the match of the century. The bout to end all bouts. The main event. In this corner, we have that scrappy, mushy muscle the *heart*. And in the corner to my left, its archnemesis—the ever-over-analyzing, over-reaching, over-overing *head*. Get ready for a smackdown, folks. My hero is bringing all the hurt. The hugs. The humor. The hope.

— Eric Morago

*I'm a war of head versus heart
And it's always this way
My head is weak, and my heart always speaks
Before I know what it will say*

— Death Cab for Cutie, "Crooked Teeth"

Do or do not; there is no try.
— Yoda, *The Empire Strikes Back*

The Day Before Rock and Roll
AKA The Pat Boone Special
AKA White Devil Music

You sat on the park bench
humming a safe melody.
Your tempo was steady and reliable.
Your shirts were ironed
and tucked in. You crossed the street
in the lines. You colored
in the lines. You used the word
colored in the lines. Bluebirds
and squirrels helped you do your dishes.
You totally won the war. Your heart
was a plush metronome. You drank
whole milk and smoked a pipe.
You said there's nothing better than
meatloaf. You were white
bread and butter. You were
saccharine. You were rock
candy at the state fair. You skipped.
You whistled. You made sure
that women knew their place.

But there was something in the air
that felt itchy. You heard reverberation
in every hammer and anvil.
Your hips started moving
with intent reserved for
harlots in boudoirs. You realized
you can't spell *abandon*
without *a band*. You wanted to carve
a slice of savage breast. You were
introducing jump blues to the Ozarks.
Ducks to tigers.
You could tell that time and space
were having a spat and things were
going to be jagged soon. Things
were going to be electric.
Percussive. People were about
to speak in tongues. In code.

You filtered out the rough air.
Your chest was a bellows.
The campfire was getting
restless. It was the time
to show a little ankle. Roll
up your sleeves. Time to use
desktops as bongos. You did this
for a girl. For a boy. For the thrill
of the ride. The bayou was calling
you. The juke joint was calling
you. The clock had just struck
11:59. Your fingers were on the B,
the A, the D chord.

What screeched out of the amp next
was an adrenalin sonic cocktail
tattooed on your libido. What happened next
was all of your *wop-bop-baloobop-wah-bop-bam-boom* tomorrows.

The Midnight Hour + The Art of Waiting

I followed the instructions on the record
and waited until the midnight hour.
Your love came tumbling down
in a cumulus avalanche.
There was no one else around—
no witness to the way your love
made its way into pillows and t-shirts
and summer dresses.

In this, the most midnight of hours,
your love began to shine.
like a new car, fresh off the lot. Your love
had that new car smell.
It had headlights that I froze in.
The stars did come out to attend
this grudge match of Twinkle vs. Eyes,
dressed in their office casuals
and hoping for a big box-office finish.

And you did all things you said you would.
You took me. You held me.
Then you began to do all the things you told me:

Short list of things to do:
Bring moonbeams home in a jar,
keep a light on at the dark end of the street,
show a little respect (but just a little bit).

And now, in the hour that was hugged by 11
and 1, this all seemed more like a close encounter.
Like a quick abduction, a sighting.
The pictures I took could have been doctored.
No one fireflies themselves that luminous.

So the horn section faded out,
the kick drum skipped away, playground ready.
All the lights and tumble packed up.
It was down to the way the moon flickered off of midnight
and the hiss and pop of the vinyl at the end of the song.

ss-tsk, it whispered, *sss-tssssk*.
The needle never leaving that last groove.
Diamond and petroleum wax whispering rhythms
that sounded like infinite patience,
like waiting twenty-three hours for the next
sixty minutes, for making it all the way to the middle,
for the whisper and crackle of this magic moment:
ss-tsssk. ss-tsssk. ss-tsssk.

1984

I have just turned 14.
It is my birthday party, a spring evening.
All the close homeboys are there:
Chris, Tom, Jeff, Andy, John, Mike. My folks decide to go out to the movies
so we, the lads, can wreak havoc—
Havoc being watching whatever's on this Home Box Office network, or this
sexy new MTV station.

We're eating pizza, drinking orange soda, talking about Lisa G. or whoever
we have our gangly crushes on.
One of the guys gives me that new Van Halen tape. The one with "Jump"
and "Hot for Teacher" on it.
I'm excited to play it. I hear it's kinda raunchy.

So, we're watching *Friday the 13th Part 2* when Andy busts out the surprise
of the night:
Two cans of beer.
This is Greendale, Wisconsin, and I am a kid who plays Dungeons and Dragons
for fun, so understand that this is the craziest thing I have done ever.

We're passing the beers around.
Only three of us are drinking.
I certainly am, because, hey, I'm 14 today.
Pizza, naked breasts on HBO, and beer sips
are my God-given right now.

I haven't had a lot of this weird tasting swill when my head starts feeling fuzzy
and fun. And then I start thinking, very swiftly, and in Technicolor:

When will I finally get kissed? Should I tell my friends that my buddy
from Church Camp wrote me a letter and told me he was gay?
Does that make me gay?
What did I do to Lisa G. to make her stop talking to me? Just because she runs track now.
This Van Halen tape is cool.
I wonder what my charisma score is in real life?
Ooh, they got killed in the movie while doing it.
This movie is awesome.
Man, do I like beer.
Man, do I like Yoda.
Why am such a weirdo?

The front door opens, and my parents waltz in, announcing their return.
Andy grabs the beers and takes them outside
via the big sliding doors we have off of our family room.
I eat some pizza really fast.

My folks look at our shitty poker faces with one eyebrow raised, suspicious,
but having no proof of chicanery.
Andy has chucked the beers into the field.
No more sips for me tonight.

I have experienced the thrill of the forbidden on May 23, 1984,
this the beginning of Year 14.
I will do things much more reprehensible as the years pass,
but this is still pure and perfect.
I kind of want to run outside into the field, find the beer-soaked earth,
and kiss it dry,
then go back inside and draw comics about me and Lisa G.
until the bumblebees in my head put me to sleep.

Instead, we watch the rest of the movie.
The bumblebees stay quiet.
That night, I fall asleep on my Star Wars sheets listening to Side One
of my new cassette. Tonight, I get up,
and nothing gets me down.

1996 Was a Great Year in Music; Relationships, Not So Much

Ready or Not
Of course we leapt in heart first. We were emotional daredevils.

Crash into Me
It sent shockwaves all over my terrain. I unbuckled my seatbelt and waited for impact.

I Believe I Can Fly
You were the best flight instructor, and before I knew it, all the buildings were tiny and touching down was impossible.

No Diggity
I was this cliggity close to telling you that I liggity loved you. You tied up my tongue that miggity much.

Lovefool
When you were my only focus, bad decisions were made. I was supportive to a fault. It was hard for you to dance when I was stepping on your feet.

If It Makes You Happy
And sometimes the word yes is said so much it becomes reflex, becomes burden, becomes shackles.

Guilty
I knew I was holding you back, even while standing on the sidelines cheering you on. I should have lost the megaphone, cancelled the laser show.

Tha Crossroads
And so here we stood, and I contemplated making a deal with the devil.
I could tell that our maps were drawn differently.

Standing Outside a Broken Phone Booth with Money in My Hand
"I gave her my heart and she gave me a pen," said one of the great philosophers. I echoed it to myself because you didn't need to watch that movie again.

Ironic
Define a writer who can never seem to say what he means.

Sleep to Dream
Sometimes two bodies in a bed go through the motions, become no more than throw pillows. Sometimes the pillows no longer offer support.

Sucked Out
When the talk finally happens, the air in the room is the first to leave.

Where It's At
The aftermath put me on a small island with a busted radio and half a paddle. The ocean liners dot the horizon. Not of one of them would ever think to steer their way towards the turbulence.

Novocain for the Soul
I got a prescription that was guaranteed to numb me. It was administered 100 proof. It stopped working every morning when the room was too big.

Naked Eye
By now, to look at me, you'd see someone rebuilt. Someone who's risen above. I have become the master of the fine stitch. I know what to wear to hide the scars.

Pepper
May we find a time where we don't think of what we did to overwhelm each other, but how for a few shakes, made each other better. Enhanced what was already full of promise.

Barely Breathing
Please do not mistake my beautiful shade of almost blue for me holding my breath. I will thank you though, for training me to exhale.

Wannabe
I'll tell you what I want. What I really, really want. For us to be able to speak each other's names without it sounding faintly like a curse. For one door to close and another to open, without anyone getting their fingers caught in the frame. For the past to finally taste like nostalgia.

romeo & juliet are together in eternity

& it is a big house.
all of the windows are fogged up
but who needs to look outside
when everything they need
exists within these walls.

romeo starts singing a john mellencamp song.
he sings *let it rock let it roh-ohl,*
let the bible belt come and save my soh-oh-ohl,
and he belly-laughs as he refills his glass
from the fountain of wine in the foyer.

juliet leafs through a book about giants
and wonders what size they are in here.
how big is a giant in eternity? contemplate further later
she scrawls in her eternity journal.
she is learning to make sorbet.
eternity has the best raspberries.

romeo wonders if he is bored
or maybe just about to make a breakthrough.
the last breakthrough involved knifes and poison,
so he hopes this one is less inconvenient.

juliet looks at romeo's lithe, 15-year-old form.
he will always look like this, erection at the ready.
she will always have boy band posters on her wall.
they will always have the same awkward early teen sex.
but since they do not know anything else, their sex
is all john mellencamp and sorbet.
they are raspberry pink houses.

do you think we'll ever leave this house, she asks,

    do we really need to, he counters.

I'm a little wary of getting everything we want, honey, she says,
it seems like the other shoe is dropping any day now.
like like like that one twilight zone episode.

julie, how do you know the twilight zone?

romey, how do you know john mellencamp?

good point.

romeo turns on the radio.

they're singing songs about us, baby! we've made it!

juliet stares at the radio dial and
makes her breakthrough.

these songs, babe,

the tears start. she wonders if they are ever gonna stop.

*these songs. they're all
so sad.*

The Last Three Viewings

I've said over and over again that the movie adaptation
of time-bending musical *The Last Five Years,*

the story of a declining relationship told from its start to its finish
(or finish to start, really, depending on who's singing),

may not be the perfect film to watch on a first date. I say this, and yet
I have watched it on a first date more times

than I care to count. I tell myself and my date
it is because the structure of the musical is

ground breaking. Cathy's songs start with the aftermath
of the divorce and careen backwards in time

to the successful first date. Jamie's songs go from successful first date
to *I went downtown and closed the bank accounts.*

It is the definition
of insanity, to expect the next first date

to be the last first date when the same
orchestrated glimpse of poorer days

continues to be screened as some dysfunctional
litmus test, the death knell of this new

(but soon-to-be-old) pairing. I can't remember if it was
Shakespeare or Roger Rabbit who said

*How do I love thee? Let me count the ways
I will bring the house down—*

and not in the sense of a great performance of a sad musical.
When I say *bring the house down,* I mean watch the walls

collapse inward, the roof torn off this motherfucker,
all due to the uneven foundation on which it sits.

This foundation that has been sabotaged by rabbits
burrowing underneath it. I used to think the rabbits

were made of Heineken and two-dollar shots of whiskey.
I used to think the rabbits needed too much attention

and were just acting out.
It is only recently that I have looked closer at the rabbits,

and by god, they are
me. They are me in a bunny suit singing,

*I've got a singular sensation/
things are moving too fast*

when I should be easing into promises about the next ten minutes
but because I have my floppy ears so far up my hutch,

I start my relationships with the end.
I can bend five years into months, or weeks, if I'm feeling ambitious.

When I am this skittish, it's fight or flight
and I can't leap to conclusions fast enough.

So there I was, in the bunny suit again, trying to act
like I didn't know where this was headed.

Trying to act like I didn't sing these songs twice a day
like medicine to salve my rabbit heart

and that I won't sing them again, even when I am happy as a lark.
The goths had it right:

Line up those sad songs in advance
and wait for the second act.

I am rebuilding, but I am still hurting.
I am moving too fast, but a miracle could happen.

Remember the time you said I don't think I can do this
and I said okay let's do this

and you said I love these playlists but slow down
and I said oh cool I will make you a playlist

and you said when this stops being fun, we stop
and I said when did this stop being fun

and we said *you're not the only one who's hurting here*
I don't what the hell is left to do

and we should've started with a happier ending
we should've taken a left turn at Albuquerque

we should just have just shut up and fucked like bunnies
we should have left this night clean and quiet

I have said this more times than I care to count.
I have watched this first date over and over again

wrapped up inside that one perfect kiss:
a goodbye, a tomorrow, a shaky foundation

making way for breaking ground.

Ghazal Amour

Dear Diary, Poems are dumb. Ghazals
are the worst of all. But here's one I love.

There is nothing more rewarding
than spending time with one I love.

I like a room full of people sometimes,
but our time one on one, I love.

This is not a competition,
and if it was, we both already won. I love

the stupid names we have for each other,
like *pirate of amour*. My one-eye love.

You are the captain of my soul,
and I am your first mate with one *aye*, love.

There are a million names for how this works,
but for me there is only one: I love.

Oh, Diary, I know I'll find that special girl,
but until then the mirror shows me the one I love.

Depress Play AKA Wear Your #$&*% Mask

And these days / we wake up and plug in the holiday lights / because it makes us / a little happier / look up fun face masks online / find one that looks like a stack of cassettes / say "I used to have that album on tape" / name off all the artists from their spines / Schooly D / Eric B and Rakim / Jody Watley / Nice and Smooth / Nu Shooz / think to ourselves, what was that jam? / Remember: *I-I-I Can't Wait* / do the synthesizer break with your mouth, sounding like a chipmunk / laugh too loud for 6 AM / think about young people being nostalgic / for the Eighties / long for the virtual community of San Junipero / a fictional sunny Eighties paradise / a throwback / but Black Mirror is now realer than we ever thought / the song title now would be / *I-I-I Have To Wait Because This World, Like My Loneliness, Is Killing Me* / which is not nearly as catchy / doesn't fit into a meme / we've tried / but at least the holiday lights look nice / at least our uncertainty about everything is amplified by everyone / in our bubble / *in our bubble, we always stay up late / in our bubble, something ray-dee-ates!* / we sing to ourselves as we long for California / and its narcissistic love ballads to California / a flashback / to friends we found who were all travelers / hitchers with headshots / cowboys with callbacks / actors slash singers slash models / another Island of Misfit Toys / and now / landlocked and blue / on red dirt / we are just an island / and we never cry / not when we can shield ourselves in lyrics / that we first heard on tape / *these are the days*, we shakily sing, *we'll remember.*

Warning Signs, or Dissecting the Spotify Playlist Post Break-Up
A found poem

I'm singing this song for you. This is your song. These arms of mine. These aching, yearning, needing, empty arms.

Dance with me. Slow dances. Dance me til the end of love. My angel. Hallelujah. This will be the answer to my prayer. Please come back. Never leave. I hope and I pray. My heart, my foolish heart. A straight line down through the heart. Be still my heart.

We can be together. Let it be me. I want you. I need you. You're all I need to get by.
Hallelujah. Hallelujah. A cold and broken hallelujah.

I'm so lonesome. My baby. My love. My baby love. Your sweet voice. Your eyes. Can't remember if they're green or they're blue. Going back to blue. Almost blue. Ain't nothing like the real thing. God only knows. I need you. I want you. I need my girl. You love, love, love, and then you die. I'd die without you. I gotta have you. I have nothing if I don't have you. You are so beautiful to me. We can give it time. Maybe we should take it slow. I will wait for you.

No one's gonna love you like I do. They won't love you like I love you. I hear in my mind all this music. Every pop song on the radio is suddenly speaking to me. When we kiss. When you hold me. I realized that I need you. All I want is you. Will you stay with me? Will you still love me tomorrow? Don't worry, baby. Baby, don't worry, you know that you got me. I'll stand by you. I wanna hurry home to you. I'm so sorry for everything. We'll hold each other soon.

I wanna hold your hand. I'm a little drunk and I need you now. I've built my life around you. Gonna love you til I die. Don't dream it's over.

Take a look at me now.

Save me.

You'll Accomp'ny Me (after Bob Seger)

You're an orchestra when you speak
of the future; of art and community
and what family means, both in the literal
and the ones we create, etching the notes
of *together* on the sheet music in our chests.

You're Stradivarius and Les Paul and
Moog and Zildjian, all sorts of twang
and flutter, crash and sweet fill. All I have
is this untrained ball of karaoke
in my throat. I strain to keep up with
the way you symphony through it all.

But soon, this voice will go stronger.
I'm warming up, learning the space
in between you and I that defines
harmony. There are octaves of undefined
possibility in our song.

I'm paying attention to this tempo,
this sophisticated rhythm, this
arrangement. Soon I will open my mouth
and have the right notes to celebrate
us. I'll stand on the edge of the stage
and croon the nuances of this collaboration.

Someday, just around the corner,
our song will leave my lips
full of funny valentines and good mornings.
And someday, lady, your arms outstretched
like harp, like six-string miracle;
someday, lady—
you'll accomp'ny me.

Night Moves (after Bob Seger)

I woke last night to the sound of thunder.
How far off? I sat and wondered.
Started humming a song from 1962,
and loaded up a box with all my kitchen essentials.

It is always a challenge to sneak out
of your currently rent-overdue apartment
when the neighborhood is an insomniac
and you are as graceful as clubfoot ballet.

But when you are faced with eviction
and your wallet is flatter than Ohio,
it's time to get your ninja on
and load up your stuff

into the back of your friend's Honda Civic.
Goddamn, do I have a lot of books.
Goddamn, books sure are heavy.
No time to flip through the pages of

the journal you found from seven years
ago, when you were eager and clumsy
with the pen. No time to revel in each
tchotchke you grab off of the shelves.

This is stealth shame motivation.
This is quit before you get fired.
The futon will have to stay, as will
that big-ass TV that doesn't suit

your new hobo lifestyle. You lock
the door for the last time, take a
deep breath, and plot the romance
of couch surfing and job hunting.

This was just a house, you tell yourself,
this was never home. You will not
miss the random sound of gunshots
or the collapsing ceilings. You climb

into the car and watch the house shrink
into the black; pull your jacket a little
tighter to your vagabond heart and feel
the beginnings of a chill, *with autumn closing in.*

When You Are Filling Out Job Applications by Hand

When you are filling out job applications by hand,
you hope your handwriting doesn't look like a serial killer's.
That your comic book style lettering will make the bosses
like you. That it has charm and quirky boyish good looks.

There are no histrionics in your voice
when you say *I am willing to do anything*.

When you are filling out job applications by hand,
you hope the letters don't look shaky.
That they don't somehow blur the line between nervous
and detox. That the letters don't betray you.

When you are filling out job applications by hand,
you are acutely aware that this is not a gig
that scrutinizes your twenty-year work history.

You just want to say,
All of this information is already on my resume
and
What does it matter where I went to high school.
but instead, you say
I am willing to do anything.

You sold your pride for bus money.
You ate your sense of worth for breakfast.
You breathe in lungs full of repetition
and exhale wisps of hope.

You do not say *I am willing to do anything*
within reason.

You hope the ink does not blot
or run out.
When you are filling out job applications by hand
the last thing you need
is to watch your please-pick-me words
fade on the page, the ghost of better paychecks,
the Braille that spells out
almost.

When you are filling out job applications by hand,
horseshoes and hand grenades
won't even give you the time of day.
It's cooking Dollar Store style
and having to split the cost of the cheap beer.
It's cutting your own hair
and meditation as medicine.
You are willing to do anything.

You have been on the other side
of that clipboard, of that manager scanning through
your last twenty years reduced to dates
and locations; the pen clicking in their hand
like Morse code for *judgement*. You want
to hear a yes so badly. You swallow profanities,
smile, and nod.

When you are filling out job applications by hand
it does not mean you are less.
It does not mean you are expendable.
You are doing a grown man's work.
Dotting your I's, crossing your T's.
You are creating a paper trail
for survival.

Cooking for One

When cooking for one, I marinate two chicken breasts, one for now and one for tomorrow, but I always make too much pasta.

Ah well, save it for later, I say, *at least you're not doing TV dinners,* I say, *no microwave for you,* I say, and so I sit here with this bowl of pasta as big as my head. As big as a mailbox. I make a mailbox of pasta and ask, *guess who's coming to dinner,* and currently my Hillbilly Jim action figure has not answered with a headcount.

So I check the mailbox and it is full of pasta and the UPS guy drops off all the extra pasta that I've made in the past year, and now there are bowls of penne stacked up to the top of the lamp, towers of tartelle, a river of fettucine flowing across my porch like the Mississippi River, starting one strand thin and growing and growing until it flows into the ocean of spaghetti and angel hair, until I am swimming through ziti and tagliatelle, until I find refuge on the curly shores of the Isle of Cavatappi. Until I build a fence made of Fusilli to keep out the savage meatballs.

I think I'm bleeding all over the screw shapes, *but no, that's not blood, that's sauce. Maybe if I make enough sauce this situation will calm down,* I say. *Maybe if people are more focused on the sea of marinara, they won't notice that I am not wearing chain mail, but a suit made out of orzo,* I say. But the trail of pasta is always going to lead back to my boiling cauldron.

And now, the two chicken breasts have rallied an army of marinated warriors in my absence, squawking, *cooking for one, cooking for one,* and I don't know if they're mocking me or if this is a life lesson about taking on too much.

I once thought leftovers were a good thing, that I was being frugal, but now all this pasta and chicken and sauce is growing cold and singing lyrics like *reheating means you're the loneliest, leftovers left for the homeliest,* and I scream *PASTA YOU'RE NOT THE BOSS OF ME* and I look to Action Figure Hillbilly Jim to back me up, but he just sits there in his eternal pose, like he was made of rubber or something.

This pasta that is everywhere around me is not a burden, I decide, even when it blocks my view at the concert, even when it is clearly using my computer simply to troll the Food Network website, even when it is terrible at being an active listener.

I will take this planet of pasta and share it because *mmmm carbs* and *oh so easy to make* and *bottoms up!* and soon the pasta will only be the size of certain government buildings and maybe a few small lakes. Then the songs of lonely and rude will turn down their volume.

And then I will switch to ramen. Because at least I know exactly what I am getting into.

Andre The Giant is Alive and Well and Working at the Circle K on 39th and Penn

I just walked in for some Vitamin Water and a pack of smokes.
I was on autopilot from a crazy night at the Red Rooster,
and I had an eight-hour shift to sleepwalk through.
That's when I saw him, barely contained in his tight corporate gear.

The nametag said *A. Roussimoff,* and I almost swallowed my tongue.
How could he be here, breathing, all seven foot four inches tall,
500-plus pounds? Didn't the masses recognize him? His swarthy
sideburns, his shadow cast imposingly over the rack of beef jerky?

I wanted to say so much to him. Tell him that *Wrestlemania 3*
was a lynchpin in my adolescent life. That his feud with Jake Roberts
was money. Hell, to see if he'd rhyme like Fezzig if I said

No more rhymes now! I mean it!

I said nothing. Grabbed an energy drink from the cooler. Tried not to stare
as I picked out what variation of Cheez-It I would use to settle the stomach.

He now sported a moustache over his broad caveman visage.
His curls were more salt than pepper now.
He had an open bottle of Grey Goose on the counter next to him.
I imagined that no one would have the gall to tell him
that he couldn't. I also imagined that if they did, he might
deliver a slap to their chest with his encyclopedia mitts.

I immediately regretted asking for the pack of Camel Turkish Golds
when I saw him gingerly bend down to grab them from the bottom row.
The cigarettes in his enormous hands looked more like a matchbook.
He had to use a pencil to poke at the register keys,
and the Yellow No.2 resembled a toothpick
as his thumb and forefinger struggled to clutch it.

My mind was racing. My brain was screaming, *Andre! You are a legend!*
You deserve so much better! Circle K will never appreciate you, Hall of Famer!

He looked at me, spilled my loose change onto the counter,
and croaked, "Don't worry, boss. Your hangover will go away soon enough."
He laughed like a bullfrog megaphone. My heart plummeted.

Andre lumbered over to the soda fountains, yanked a small cup
from the stack and poured a trickle of vodka into it. He slid it
across the counter to me.
"Hair of the Dog, boss," he bellowed.
I thanked him meekly, and as I shuffled out the double doors,
felt light-headed and surreal as I stumbled into the workday.
I never saw him again; was told he transferred to another store
in Norman. I couldn't bring myself to find him there.

I went to sleep on the night of my giant sighting,
dreaming that Andre was the special after-hours guest
of the now-defunct JR's BBQ Restaurant,
surrounded by slabs of meat, buckets of barbecue sauce,
and an oversized mug of beer, kept full all meal long.

I hoped that he went to sleep that night on a big wooden table,
content to know some form of normal for just a few hours,
numb on an alcohol cloud
and dreaming of large women.

Plancha

In the squared circle,
when a wrestler launches themselves
at another wrestler,
usually from a turnbuckle
or slingshot over the top rope,
it is called a *plancha*.
Chests bump and gravity takes over.

It's about momentum.
Using your weight to propel things forward.
Advancing the storyline.
It's about hearing your vocal cue
and hurling yourself into arms.
About trusting that you will be protected.

Armed with this knowledge, know too
that stumbling into you was never an act.
It was easy to take a running leap,
to surrender to the tumble.

I demand a rematch.
I demand a receipt.
I want the breathlessness of a *huracanrana*,
the impact of a tornado suplex.
I am airplane-spin dizzy for this.

I know; you're the hometown favorite,
and I may never win.
I'm willing to risk it all for one more try.
You're so talented, so precise,
that you make me feel,
for a few adrenaline-soaked heartbeats,
that I really can
fly.

Worse Than My Bite

1. In Oklahoma City,
when you are a pedestrian,
you become accustomed to the sound
of dogs barking.

I've long since stopped trying to figure out
whether they are welcoming me,
or warning me,

City boy, we are not impressed.
Take your shiny shoes and show tunes
from whence they came.
That's right, we said whence.
Don't think that we're not booksmart.

2. There are a lot of dogs in Oklahoma City.
They are family out here in a way they could never be
in the grid that I came from some few thousand miles west.
Even the surliest one out here just wants a little attention.
They're love-bullies at worst.

I've since grown accustomed to seeing them
at the bars I go to, wandering from table
to booth, a few seconds of time at each,
figuring out who's got the affection this minute.
Boy, do I relate. Find me at a party, and
I cannot sit still until someone
is scratching me behind my ears.

3. I wonder if I should get a dog.
People see me around small children,
playing all their reindeer games,
following all the rules of their magic spells,
and say I'd be a great dad.
I'm thinking I should start small.
A dog and I could have unconditional love contests.

4. I just wanna be your dog.

5. I'm in training to become a good dog.
I know how to sit. How to stay.
I know I tend to run full stop
towards people who treat me right.
Sometimes I need a good "down, boy"
to reel me in. I just want some lap time.
We all do, so come on.

Throw me a bone.

If You Missed the House Concert

The porch was alive, bristling and acoustic.
Voices cut into the night,
sweet siren and definitive foghorn.
Dogs and cats were noticed and loved.

Hands were held.
Ears were arched forward towards reverb
and words that spilled all over the deck.
There was awkward and giggle
and the night air took it all in,
smirking voyeur.

Oh, sure, there were flashes of phones,
sneaky texts against the moonlight.
There were wisps of conversation
leaking out the sides of the lawn.

There were bathroom breaks
and stops into the kitchen
and a few who were only there for the spirits.

But the wine was listening.
The cigarettes were fireflies craning to burn
in rhythm with the hand claps,
the foot stomps, the moments of singalong.

The glass jar marked *suggested donation*
was a scrumptious salad,
a bouquet telling the breeze
that the new universal healthcare
was in the key of just what we needed.
The medicine was plucked and blessed
and as ripe as the tomatoes sliced juicy for lips.

As we swayed out into the sweet air,
we dodged twigs and trampled red dirt.
We laughed and were chivalrous.
The wind carried the music with us.

How can a world contain so many bursts of necessary,
so much fire and memory? These are questions
that we have learned to keep in our hope chests.
We are leaving the answers in the grass,
in the gardens, behind that mastodon of an RV.

We are grateful that there are still nights
that can salve our smarting hearts.
I am grateful that fingers on strings and chanteuse throats
keep my goofy romance furnace lit.

Now all I want to be when I grow up
is a porch.

The First Attempt: 11/1/11

1. You throw out all the trophies of war first.
The same glass and aluminum brand names
that you mocked frat boys and rednecks
for wearing on their promotional t-shirts.
The same brands you sneered at hipsters
for donning on their cruddy trucker caps.

2. You are now Statler and Waldorf.
You sit in the balcony and make fun
of the Muppets who are actually achieving things.

3. Maybe you should take up smoking again.
Maybe just cloves.
Maybe just hookahs.
Maybe you should take bong hits to the face
to drown out the fucking annoying chatter
that is ninety-seven percent of humanity.

4. You drink things that remind you vaguely
of what you used to drink.
Grape soda.
Cream soda.
It is important to feel full.

5. CM Punk is your favorite wrestler.
CM Punk, when he was a bad guy,
was the leader of a faction named
The Straight Edge Society. CM Punk
is straight edge in real life. CM Punk
calls himself the Voice of the Voiceless,
the Best in the World. You wear
his T-shirt and no longer feel that the X
on your chest is ironic.

6. Your ribcage is a recovering alcoholic.
You are taking your angel wings out of the shot glass.
Nothing feels like an original thought.

7. Endorphins are the new booze.
You cry at the end of every Rocky movie.

8. When someone first offers to buy you a beer
and you say you've stopped drinking,
they ask you *when did you quit*
and you tell them *I am one month sober*
and you watch eyebrows raise
as an amalgam of shock and something else—
doubt? relief? trails across their half-smile.
The words **GOOD FOR *YOU!***
spoken a little too loud. You can almost hear
the bets being taken. You wonder what the spread is.

9. You start holding funerals.
Here lies the Life of the Party.

10. This is a break-up.
You wonder if you can learn
to live with it, or if it's best to keep your
distance. You miss the way that your first beer
slowly loosened the pressure valve.
You know that you have never won an argument
with alcohol. You know you never will.

11. Everything pierces your chest plate
like Uma Thurman adrenaline shots.
You are impatient. Your head hurts.
The world keeps throwing drunks
in your path. You find yourself uncomfortable
around their stagger and blur. They look
too much like mirrors.

12. So you're sober
and everything is louder
and sharper
and who cares except maybe you
and your desire to feel in 3-D again
and this must get easier
and the only thing you know unequivocally is that
this poem will never be over.

Dear Poet More Successful Than I Am,

While you were off collaborating with DJ ZIBBYZAB
and acting opposite hunk-throb MACGREGOR THOMAS-TILSON
I was out writing poems in notebooks!

I went down to the XEROX STORE and stuck my poems in their machine
and stapled them by hand.
DIYFTW!

Not like your YouBox animation shows (voiced by comedian FLEEK EPIPHANY)-
No, my sweet little muffin tops...
I've been in the goddamned trenches!

There are no CHEESE PLATTERS in the trenches.
No Dancer In The Dark Matches to warm up the crowd.
We warm up the crowd by lighting our poems on fire
with our plentiful POET CIGARILLOS.
WE DO NOT VAPE, POSERS. We are E-Free. We are Fr**.

I do not go inside POD CASTLES and generate HIT POINTS.
I collate my poems 20 at a time
and I throw them at people. Art is supposed to HURT.

I'm crafting a whole new set of poems out of BAR NAPKINS
and scotch tape. Art is supposed to be FLEETING.

How dare you learn DISCIPLINE years before I did,
when I was just happy to be paid in FREE BOOZE.

How dare you be born of focus and knowing what you want.
Damn me for my errant liver and its classic taunts.

But it's all good because my HATERADE IS 100 PROOF!
There is NO POETIC RAGE like that of a sober straight white male!
I am punk rock and you are one of those 80's New Wave bands like TIME CAN TRAVEL!

I am rhyming in the park and you've turned into into a commercial calamity
like YOUNG SASSYFRASS and his hit single GROOVE JEWELS (IN MY
PANTS)!

My words were beaten against ROCKS and made smooth
by mountain rapids lapping against their hides!

My words aren't connected to the FANDANGLE APPSITE
or gulped down like that SNAZZLE JUICE you posers pose with!
I don't get paid with royalties or contracts–
I hand my patron a fistful of dimes
and make them RENDER ME ASLEEP.
Art is supposed to be senseless and ARTISTIC.

Is that a poem or did you just endorse a soft drink?
Is that a poem or did you just land on the moon and
GRAFFITI TAG BUZZ ALDRIN?

I am so MAD at you.
I do NOT know how to DIRECT THIS ANGER.
I am thinking of switching to puppetry.
I fear becoming so small that my words can only be heard by
ANTS and MEN THE SIZE OF ANTS.
Ant-Man would be a welcome audience.

You are either everything I never wanted
or some kind of goddamned perfect GENIUS.

I'll need to conduct a clinical study.

Take me with you.

I Love How You Love

When you are in love,
when you, specifically, are in love,
you rewrite your journals all over again
from Page One, because this time
is going to be the big bang rainbow fireworks ending.
This is going to the love that Muppets sing of
in inspirational, non-gender specific terms.

And I have been there a dozen times myself.
Because when someone is brave enough
to take a chance on people like us, to throw
themselves headfirst into our swing set emotions,
it is the best action movie we have ever written.

You squeeze all the happiness out of every statement,
not in an exhausting way, but more in the sense
that a statement like "spring is coming" morphs into
"I am a bloom, a greening leaf, all of my chlorophyll
is leaning into your sunbeam arms"
and truthfully, we're all better for it.
It makes me feel that I'm not a lunatic
for still hanging on to hope. And some day soon

some lucky girl is going to walk by my windshield
and she'll like my blinkers and poof, we will be
a two-car garage. Because you and I could have ended
like a car crash but the night we parted you took
me to the body shop and got me a new paint job.

You showed me that sometimes, as fun as all
of the volumes of past-lover-memoirs can be
to peruse, sometimes, captain, you gotta put them
back in the hope chest and grab a new notebook.

Here's to Page One. When I start there again,
may I, and may you, never have to go back.

Sailor to Mermaid, or Message No Longer in The Bottle

Hey there, Swimmy.

I'm sure it's not at all a surprise that
you taught me a valuable lesson about the sea:
there are the maps we plan,
the maps we follow,
and the maps that are created in our wake.

But I am weary of sailing.
The *yo ho ho* is played out.
The bottle of rum has lost its charm. I have invested
in a tiny lighthouse. It's good
for keeping small ships safe.
It also keeps me looking for you.

I am thinking of renovating it.
Building it up so it can cast a longer light.

I don't know why. My friends think me crazy,
sitting home each night, singing into seashells,
occasionally peeking out the window
to see what the light reveals.
You'd think I'd have given up by now.
You'd think I'd have stopped believing.

Water Lily, you told me once
that you are a terrible human being.

I am telling you mermaids are always
terrible human beings. But they are
exquisite mermaids. They are fierce
and empathic and they will love you
the only way they know how. Like
a warrior. Like a healer. Like someone
who never expects credit for it.

Angelfish, do you remember the first time you asked me
to come into the waves with you?
I got knocked down, I was disoriented
and I got scared.

But then I righted myself.
I found my footing.
You helped me find my strength,
or at least at you stifled your laughter.
Either way, it was appreciated.
The waves, I know now,
weren't trying to diss me.
At the time, though,
I cursed and kicked at them.
I was mad at the ocean
for being the ocean.
I see that.
I'm not afraid anymore.

Some nights I convince myself
that the silhouette across the water
is not an adventurous dolphin
or a protective mother shark.
Some nights I know unequivocally that it is.
Most nights I still believe
that maybe it's your way of checking in on me.

I don't know what any of this means
to you. I am writing this and putting it
in our old bottle. I am setting it adrift
along channels I hope you're tuned in to.
I know I haven't been out to sea
for a hot minute. I know the tides
have shifted. If you never message back,
I would not blame you.

Shellfish, it is selfish to want what you gave up.
When you throw back what practically
leapt into your arms, why on this soaking wet globe
would you expect that magic
to happen twice?

Still, I dip my toes in the water,
knowing full well what I'm doing.
I am weary of sailing
but if you called, I would set adrift immediately.
Maybe we can meet halfway.

Popeye The Sailor Ruminates on Love

Lisken.
I cants tells ya nothin' ya don'ts already know.
Wimming will be the deaths of ya if ya let em be,
but they skin also saves yer life.

I gets exasperpated when I sees perfeckly good wimming
fallin' fer the same ol' manipulashkun overs and overs,
cuz they don't feels like they gotsk the right to be equalified
with their sweetie. That's a load of jeep crap.
Olives and I are equalipated in every way. We boths take care
of me Swee'Pea, we boths go shoppifying for veggigables
and cold cucks and such, we takes turns washin' dishkes.

I yam happy as Wimpy at McDonalds when we settles on the couch
and watch our shows (She likes Wheels of Forchkun, I watches
Friday Nights Smackdowns). No, we don't always agree on everthings.
But she loves me. She wraps her pipe cleaner body
around my misk-shapen forearms and and whiskerpates my name
into me cauliflower ear. She makes me heart pitter-pat so fask
I feel dizzier then when Bluto spins me around.
When she goes away, my stomach hurts
like The Sea Hag put broken glass in me spinach.

I says to her, "Olives, I loves ya. And I wishes
I could be hooked up to a spinach IV
so's I could saves ya twenky-four hours a day."

And Olives looks at me with those raisinks for eyeballs,
and says in her prettified screech of a voice,
"Oh, Popeye. I don't WANT to be saved all the time.
Sometimes I just want to be sad or scared or in distress
so I can save myself every once in a while."

And that's when the freight trains start exclatin in me muskles
and the spinach can pops open in me chesk
and that's when I realizes, that in that momenk,
that perfeck momenk,
our loves is strong to the finnich.
And in that momenk,
I yam saved too.

Unsexy Beast: A Monstertown Personal Ad

this ain't no peach pit flower petal limb lock rubdown
no mango honey licorice whip tease bomb
dunno how to smooth sail the barry white water rapids
not no bootknockin' smack flipbedroom eye dropper

me no ultra glide velvet smog kiss bandit
never went to extra hump digital playground school
not no triple threat good musk horse pants
just a cyclops tangled fur space invader

looking for a talk nice pretty dress bombshell lass
hoping she don't scream loud run fact cop call
maybe if i razor down perfume up gargle honey
she won't be the point laugh always busy back turner

maybe we can ticket buy showtune watch cheap seats it
or candlelight spaghetti share lady tramp be
sure would like to park bench pigeon feed ice cream buy
hope if i nuzzle close extra hug she won't taser mace

girl i want won't be a trip out act a fool change maker
won't ask for tummy tuck nose job penis pump
so if you like the shiny horned purple fur almost smart
call me on my fax machine blackberry tin can string

signed,
unbringing not sexy back

Oh, Hey There, Sunshine Gnomes!

Thank you for the postcards.
At first, I couldn't read the handwriting
because I forgot how to speak sunbeam.
I've got the Rosetta Stone now and it's coming
back to me in short bursts.

I'm glad to know that you've been following
me on all the social media outlets
as well as all the wall socket outlets.
Thank you for keeping the lights on
and for trying to keep me out of the dark.

I absolutely must get the recipe
for the sparkle cake y'all made for me.
The way that the frosting tastes like
giggle-fits and moon-shadows.
It sends me something pretty.

I really appreciate that when somebody sees you
and calls you elves or pixies,
you don't feel the need to correct them.
You just slap on your party ears
or your feather cape, and say, "You got it.
Now boogie is as boogie does."

You found me at the bottom of the well,
hoisted me up on red licorice vines,
and turned on a playlist that helped me
to pour out all the sepia-tone in my gullet.
Gave me a technicolor telescope.
Taught me to speak in spectrum.

I can't thank you enough. You are all
the apologies that I tried to run from,
only to find I'd been stationed at Fort Forgive
the whole time. And I am not sorry
for hogging the love wardrobe.
I've needed to try these clothes on for a while,
to remember that they still fit.

I have some words for you,
and I hope you can bake them into torts
or seed them in barren places,
so they grow to full-size
in the yards of those who really need them:

Accept.
Yes.
Belief.
Recover.
Endure.
Best.
Shine.
Shine.

By all things glorious and redeeming,
you cute, bearded bastards—

shine.

Bedtime Story

Once upon a time,
Pear-Shaped Boy and Sparkly Girl spoke by way of tin cans connected with taut string.

They were too shy and scared to say "How much do you like me," so instead they just whispered words they liked.

"Plaster," he said.
"Elephant," she said.
"Tangent," he gasped.
"Mellifluous," she breathed.
"Inferno?" he asked.
"Tempest," she insisted.
"Jackdaw," he hinted.
"Nomenclature," she drawled.

They did this for hours until their arms got tired and their necks were sore. When he slept that night, he was Hannibal riding an elephant through a great storm.

Her dreams placed her as a great warrior princess kicking demon ass with a singing sword.

They wrote each other thank-you notes the next morning and placed them on the backs of carrier turtles. Their separate but similar reasoning was that if the sentiment could not last over the course of the turtle's journey, then it was not worth sending.

Their thank-you's were just as goofy.

Hers read, "To the professional shower singer: I would like to request David Bowie, Nas, Paul Simon, and Sarah Vaughn. Sincerely, Your Loofa."

His read, "Be wishful about what you care for. I am made of pennies."
Their collective sighs powered the kind of sailboats manned by the great explorers.
Happily,
Ever after.

Sharp

He didn't want to be made of razors.

He hadn't been touched in years.

Every so often, some girl would
look at him longingly,
lick her lips,
but it wasn't because she loved him.
It was because she hated herself.

His house was littered
with shredded love letters
and scratched-up beer bottles.

He watched *Edward Scissorhands* on loop,
knocked whiskey down his silver gullet,
and tried to dull.

Then he met the girl
who could heal herself instantly.

She looked at him differently.
Asked him to sing to her.
Said his voice was a baritone miracle.

He couldn't be more wary.

She broke him down like rust.
Trusted him like no one had before.
He loved shaving her legs.

One night, he was wrapped around her,
watching her cuts close up
as quickly as they opened.
He asked, "Why me? I hurt you every day."

She smiled and said,
"Who doesn't?"
Made some joke about how sharp he was.
He carved makeshift hearts into her thighs,
over and over.

Skyrim Keeps Me Honest

I would have tried to reconcile with you
but then I took an arrow to the knee.

I was going to apologize for my bad behavior
but then I took an arrow to the knee.

I thought it was a good idea to win you back
but then I took an arrow to the knee.

So I picked up the phone and almost dialed
but then I took an arrow to the knee.

I looked to see if I had pictures of us
but then I took an arrow to the knee.

Tried to make a list of all the good times
but then I took an arrow to the knee.

Started feeling sorry for myself in your wake
but then I took an arrow to the knee.

Thought about drinking you out of my head
but then I took an arrow to the knee.

Was going to see if I still had your emails
but then I took an arrow to the knee.

So I considered building an effigy
but then I took an arrow to the knee.

Mustered every last feeling I had about us
but then I took an arrow to the knee.

I thought you hurt me in brand new ways,
but then I took an arrow to the knee.

The best advice I've ever taken
was when I took an arrow to the knee.

So if you see me limping down the street,
it's because I took an arrow to the knee.

And if I think of ambling back your way,
I'll take another arrow to the knee.

Stop Me if You've Heard This

A werewolf, a woodcutter, and an encyclopedia salesman walk into a bar. It's a great set-up for a joke I have no punchline to. I like to riff, to start stories that have no end, hoping I'll conjure something magical. I talk a better game than I play. That doesn't mean that I won't give the game a go. I'll try over and over until I get it right. I am the close in horseshoes and hand grenades. I am the reason tutorials were invented. I don't remember recipes. It's always a splash of this, a dollop of that. I'd rather write it out in Sharpie than find a font. At least I know the reliability of my own handwriting. It's the same reason I would always start drawing comic books and never finish them. I can't create stories because I don't want my characters to fight. I am no good at conflict but it always seems to find me. Tension knocks on my door with pamphlets asking for a moment of my time. I look for release at the bottom of a shot glass. I try to sell them on my words. I try to bury the hatchet. I warn them of the monster inside. I am a werewolf. A woodcutter. An encyclopedia salesman. The punchline is me.

What do you get for someone who:

was a goofball for musicals
used to be in a band called The Get Classic Now
did laundry every other Sunday
had days of the week underpants
made pesto
loved cheese tortellini
used to be in a band called The Berlin Wallflowers
sang "My Freeze Ray" before a show to psyche up
cheated at solitaire
donated books and CDs
wouldn't throw away the lucky Chucks
laughed like a sprinkler
hogged the sheets
was all about plants
had a bookshelf full of journals
cried at the same songs every time
used to be in a band called the Crossfire Hurricanes
sang in bed
danced in the shower
hated to do the dishes
loved vacuuming
had a plastic wobbly hula girl on the dashboard
was obsessed with *Fables* comics
used to be in a band called Plato's Symposium
used to be in a band called Do The Math
used to be in a band called Sugar Sweet and the So Are You's
used to be in a band called Heartbreak Soup
trusted like a puppy
had bad nightmares
sat across the table, nibbled a breadstick, said things like
I'm thinking of incorporating more kicking into the stage show.
You know, like David Lee Roth.
played bass like a black widow, fingers crawling across the thick coiled steel
invented Cuddle Sundays
went to work on a bike
had a parachute tattoo to remind her that it's okay to jump
made you feel better
was all made up

Band Geek

The tuba sits in the back of the band room,
brass fumble and elephant lung.
He knows his place is to be backbone to the melody.
He is the two and the four of the tempo, bass clef bashful
and just wanting to be part of the dance.

He looks at the back of a lot of heads
that rarely turn to listen to his harrumph and plod.
And there she is, rows in front of him,
the clarinet. The stuff of sonatas, sleek,
smooth embouchure and trill.
He knows she isn't perfect; he's heard the squeaks
and breathiness from her section before.

And he sees her admiring the saxophone
when that guy begins to work his way around the room
weaving jazz bop seduction songs.
There's always a saxophone that gets first look.
All collar up, Coltrane and Parker pedigree.

Someday, he muses, *someday I will meet her,*
somewhere far away from these horrible uniforms
and John Philips Sousa parade marches. There
will be no sheet music then, no predetermined tempos.
They will not have their instruments in front of them
and although he still may have the confidence of a tuba player,
she will see something solid in him
that a million saxophones never wanted to provide.

Their conversation will become trills and low tones.
An awkward waltz with two unlikely players.
Someday she will weave melodies for him soft and perfect,
and he will do his level best to remain her backbone.

WWE Manager Paul Heyman and I Go to Hot Topic Because It's BOGO T-Shirt Weekend
after Ellyn Touchette

Even before we enter the store, when we are still by LensCrafters, scream-o music throbs from Hot Topic's retail orifices, making small children uncomfortable and forcing old people to cross to the other side as if these Sons of Slipknot have a posse (caveat: in this mall, they very well may).

Paul chuckles and says,

This sound was cutting edge back when we had Shane Douglas drop the belt in Philly. Now it's just elevator music.

He's dressed to the nines and I couldn't feel more like a fanboy in my Daniel Bryan ballcap and nWo t-shirt, but the truth is it's Buy One Get One Free Weekend at the one place in the mall that still carries wrestling tees and really cool ones at that. Tees that a pop singer might wear when they're being Instagram Casual.

The display upfront is overflowing with those adorable POP! collectables made by Funko, the ones that look like Hello Kitty attempting cosplay—

They're ubiquitous and also a sign that you've made it.

The Architect of Extreme raises his eyebrows and beelines for them—

My kids love these, he tells me.

Dark Willow! I reply.

We hold up little Groots and Green Lanterns to show each other that we may or may not buy.

Arrrgh, Paul. I can't get caught up here. I came to find some t-shirts.

I walk in and face a wall of *Adventure Time,* Marvel Comics, and vintage logos from 90's bands.

The 19-year-old bangled employee leans on the counter looking at me, attempting customer service via mental telepathy.

I ask her, *Do you have any t-shirts that say "I'm a Paul Heyman Guy"?*

Who's Paul Heyman? she asks.

I look over to Paul with my head on a swivel. He's loading up a basket with the cutest Walking Dead bobbles you've ever seen. He's heard none of this.

I want him to set down the basket and say:

Ladies and gentlemen, my name is Paul Heyman, and I am the advocate for Rob Sturma and his shopping needs.

I want him to spend ten minutes dressing down and deconstructing the terrible floor plan executed by the assistant manager.

He only sets the basket down on the counter and says,

I'm definitely getting these, as soon as my friend is done picking out shirts. Rob, did you find anything?

I reply, *Uh, yeah. An old school Macho Man in lavender and one with a retro Bash at The Beach logo. And some Punk stuff on clearance.*

Put 'em in the basket, he tells me.

Paul, are you sure?

He insists because no one appreciates the art of the sell than Paul Heyman. *The advocate for the reigning, defending, nostalgic heavyweight man-child bargain tee champion*—and his shopping needs.

Poor Thing
For Ben Grimm

You're a rough beast with a Bethlehem slouch.
A bullet-pocked brick wall weeping.
Your footsteps are thunder gravel;
your eyelids, mechanical shutters.

How long did it take you to relearn the art of delicate?
How many shattered glasses were buried
in your reawakening? Your irreversible armor
has made you de facto warrior. It is a mantle

that weighs heavy on your granite breastplate.
Once in a great while, you channel Claude Rains
as you don fedora and trenchcoat to try to
move among the tiny. It is an exposed prestige

at best. Your clothes make you a reverse mite.
You are a rubbernecker photograph, which may be
why your best friend is someone who has the ability
to make you invisible. We always seek those

who can best complement us. And yes, you have found
love, but it eats at you with acid reflux cruelty.
Your lover without sight wrapping herself around
your enlarged beneficent heart. There is a name

for women who swoon over gargoyles. There is a name
for a man who has forgotten what it was like
when holding someone's hand didn't feel
like brushing fingertips on ochreous sidewalk.

There will be a day when peace washes over you
like irradiated skin. There will come a time
when the word *fantastic* doesn't sound like a
carnival catch phrase echoing in your canyon ears.

You reluctant soldier, you concrete angel.
You have never been simulacrum to us—
and if you believe, Ben, if you trust hard enough,
someday you will let yourself be a real boy again.

Lego Hulk Teaches Me About Life on the Last Day of 2014 via the Lego Marvel Videogame

1. There are things that only Lego Hulk can do. Look for the green handles and you will smash effectively. Press X and down goes the wall, away goes the fuel tanker.
2. There are things that only Bruce Banner can do. Sometimes you will encounter a raft that seats one. Hold the Y button. Get un-angry. Get on board.
3. Everything looks impossible, but really, everything is just made of bricks. Bricks can be smashed.
4. Press A, press A, press A, move forward.
5. It is not a contradiction to be adorable and dangerous at the same time.
6. You don't always have to take the lead. That's why Lego Iron Man is there, and Lego Spidey, and Lego Wolverine. Bring them Lego coffee. Wait for your turn. Then press A, press A, press A, all you want.
7. You are a bundle of brick and fierce. You didn't wake up like this, but you are still flawless.
8. The bricks will come. Keep on smashing.
9. You don't have to smash everything all at once. Press pause. Have lunch. Stark Tower will still be there. The Baxter Building will still be there. All of New York will freeze in place and when you return, press A like you've never pressed A before.
10. Somewhere in Oklahoma, a man-child will wait impatiently for you to download. You don't even know how much he has been waiting to meet you. The world seems safer in the trail of your irradiated purpose. Thank you for your irreverence. For your lumpy green physique. Your Lego sense of humor will wash over this man like catharsis.
11. There are things that only Lego Hulk can do. You are so necessary.

Moon Takes a Lover

to the sitting room
Moon is neither ladylike nor gentlemanly
Moon uses them/they/their pronouns

Moon grows themselves from their own ribs
Opens six cans of moonshine
Sits half in shadow
Hates the way they've eroded
Doesn't trust their reflection

Lover says *drink in your beauty*
Lover says *that's amore*

Moon thinks they are not fit
for lover
Too bright/not bright enough

Kid on ground says *ooh moon so round*
Moon curls into ball
Nurses their shine
Tries to put on a happy face for Lover

But moon is always distant

rarely full

always blue

Dry Dock (4/4/14)

You could never take 12 steps without tripping over your own feet,
but you still count days off on a calendar. *This decision is not a sentence.*

You're throwing back empty shot glasses until you remember
that you can drink in lungfuls of air on your own now.

When you live in a world where just one
becomes three becomes five becomes seven,

when your liver wakes up and curses at you in Klingon or Elvish
so that maybe you'll finally understand—

you gotta remind yourself that even Dean Martin was drinking
apple juice most of the time. And this, like the shape of your ears

or your metabolism or your weakening vision,
this is something that has always been in your bloodline.

And so maybe the world does get a little too clear these days;
beer billboards are not nearly as sexy as they are obvious,

2 AM sneaks up on you so fast, a master assassin, and all
you want is the same kind of assurance that gin brought

to your pillow. And when did they start selling Maker's Mark
on The Disney Channel?

When you tell yourself, *nobody likes a quitter,*
panic steps on your throat. Has your wit reached its end?

Did all the wobbly charm you had go on strike? You're forced
to reboot, to sip the air, slowly. Your emotions are staged

like a script split into jigsaw pieces. You're relearning your lines.
So the first time you cry when watching an undersized bearded

professional wrestler win a predetermined contest, it's partly because you understand his struggle. You don't miss

any of the things that you're supposed to; the feel of a cold bottle, the sting and warm throat. You don't even want to start again.

But closure has always been your biggest fear. This is the longest relationship you've ever been in. And divorcing it

is still so fucking hard.

Pep Talk

Listen up, you creaky-ass window.
I see you practicing your *woe is me* pose.
Looking in the mirror trying to conjure some raindance out of
those dusty look-pockets.
You need to quit writing these dark moon horoscopes,
the ones that start with, *We hate to say we told you so.*
It seems that what happened is you decided to empty yourself
into someone who deserved all of your sunstuff. And that's seven
kinds of sweet.
But it ain't gotta be all or nothing, you goofy this-and-that.
You have to remember that giving up too many rays puts your
whole feel factory in the shade.
And some folks just don't have the SPF to take you in proper.
Think in terms of droplets, open windows, small dollops.

Remember how super solid it was to see the lawn
after the freeze blankets took it away for a whitewash? It's like that.
Now I'm not saying you should only get warm in a seasonal fashion.
That's not practical or neighborly, Moody Pete.
There are plenty of teacups waiting for all your flavors.

But the new rule: you're always first dibs on the mixing bowl
leftovers. As it should be.
But I just wanted be her sugar cookie, you tell me,
and now she looks at me like diabetes. Well, guess what.

People move on all the time.
They lock their doors and don't forward their address.
Save your postcards for those open mailboxes anticipating
your newsletters.

I've met enough pillows inching towards you,
fluffing themselves up for storytime. I've been watching
how the notches on your grow chart keep moving higher
up the responsibility wall. You are three sparks away
from unlocking the explosion achievement. Plug back in.
Turn on the open sign.
There will always be a few stragglers that hover
before the paying customers start pouring in.
And if I put my ear to the wall

and hear the Pity Party Playlist bumpin' through your system, I'm coming in and opening a can of Get-Right on ya.

Now go out there and get gorgeous.

Tinder

1. *dry, flammable material, such as wood or paper, used for lighting a fire.*
2. *Not the dating app*

PART ONE: RED

One night, after we kissed goodbye,
my porch caught fire
from an errant spark off a cherry
hitting dry and wanting flesh.

The way to my hearth,
a wall composed solely
of tinder. Ready to burn.
Has been for a while.
These are optimal conditions
for things to blow the hell up.

This stands to reason.
There is no one in this room tonight
even remotely resembling the word
cool.

We are all flushed cheeks,
thanking God for ceiling fans.
We are hand candles.
I am drawn to you like sparks
to tinder.

PART TWO: ORANGE

As an addict, I replace
things or routines with other things
or routines. Sparkling water when
I want a drinky-drink. The adrenaline
of Scoville units to feed the buzz. A mint
when I want to set things on fire and inhale.
And best believe I am palms out
hoping for your hot hands to find me.

I am wholly aware of how much heat
you give off. I am drawn to it.
Call me Mothman.
I am trying to hover close
and not catch fire in the process.

PART THREE: WHITE

When I met you, I was the driest pile of twigs.
When I met you, you made my Zippo wheel spin.
We were combustible elements who were clearly
off the charts. Susanna Hoffs tells me to
close my eyes and give her my hand, darling,
and it is now our personal prom theme.

Sing porch fire to me
and I will melt accordingly.
You and I: the warmest receptions,
the burning home fires,
erratic, dancing,
tinder and sparks.
We look perfect in this light.

All Hail the New Ambassador of Awesome.

She mandolined-and-tambourined in through the doorway,
a strawberry sunshine shaman singing the spell for trouble.
She had pictures of wood nymphs flying out of her wallet;
was finishing checklists while whistling windchime backbeats.

She turned sharp phrases that were en garde to duel city
into pillow fight bear hugs. Turned heads
with the boomerang gut shot in her voice.
The song always came back to her.
The song brought friends, and the friends brought refreshments.

Folks, folks, and folks, there is no audition process
to become the New Ambassador of Awesome.
No voting. No scorecards.
Some humans were just born with extra diplomacy.
Some people are natural sparkle-bots.

So this is how she earned her title.
One leaf and twig at a time.
With extra scoops of elbow grease
and heaping helpings of vinyl cracklings.

And what you saw, once the sun went down,
it wasn't a trick of the lighthouse.
It wasn't sleight-of-handclaps.
She really did turn on the prayer candles
with her cornhusk laugh and her promise ringtones.

So yeah. She was as least as magic as a wave
of wonderous wands. At least as inspirational
as orgasm high-fives. Of course you fell, friend.
She was a professional trapdoor.

But, damn, could she keep torch songs
ignited. A patchwork chanteuse in the making,
unstitching your insecurity blankets
and fashioning a cape for you. Perfect fashion
for when you're rocketing back down to earth.

She is still the reason
you took flying lessons.

Some days you put her records on,
envision her two-stepping in a brandy snifter,
Singing metahuman ¾ tango,
and tuck yourself in between her voice
and the static—
Last twinkle before closing time.

Color the Night Sky

Remember the night, when you, drunk on astronomy,
showed me that the stars were multicolored in the night sky;
not just a bland, monochromatic white?
The night where I was like,
well, I was already into the stars and their shiny bravado
but now I'm all the way shook?

It's like you opened up the whole pack of Magic Markers,
showed them to this wide-eyed tourist,
and shifted his world like he was Judy Garland walking into
Technicolor for the first time.
Like it was 1954 and you turned on an RCA television
to the Tournament of Roses Parade.
Everyone in the room had to take a minute to catch their breath.

You Got Me All Giddy/Up

Today I am learning to cowboy up—
slowly sipping sarsaparilla,
holstering my best intentions
while you are Profanity Jane
galloping into this friendly ghost town
like a bat out of hell yeah.

Under the shade of your Oakley tree
I am all hat and no cattle—
a drugstore cowboy whose prescription ran out;
an empty general store.
An abandoned goldmine.

We roll up and I call you Red
and you call me Slim and we laugh
because at least one of us is right.

They have written songs about us,
my sweet tumbleweed;
etched 'em on piano rolls
and carved 'em into the backsides of banjos.
They have emptied our adventures
into one pulled note on a C harp.

The coyotes are howling in the distance.
This campfire is crackling like sarcasm.
The only spur I hear jangling is your whisper.
It sounds like the desert wind.

We sound like a new frontier.
We sound like every "go west" ballad
ever crooned by cook or by crook.
Like a wagon rumbling across uneven prairie.
Like the promise of more.

Who's Going to Drive You Home

We are not drivers.
We are soles and heels and thumbs.
We are hitchhikers
and we stumble over rocks near the curb
as we move forward at our own damn pace.

We have no idea how the hell we're going to get
from Point A to Point B.
Our phones are on the fritz.
The taxicabs are pouting
and won't come out at all.
So we make maps.
We look up the shortest route;
we sync our watches
before we lace up our shoes
and then we get to stepping.

Our shoes wear down
quickly.
Our shoes are battle transports.
Our laps are porch swings and rest stops.
We are the vagabond hearts.
We are hobos. Emotional bums.
We have panhandled for affection before.
We are mostly only human. We have been skinned knee
and whiskey blind in our aftermath. Our best intentions
sometimes slip out of our fingerless hobo gloves.

Hey, Handkerchief Annie—hop on this traincar with me.
Let's thank the smoke in the distance,
prepare for the new smoke just ahead.
Even if this track just goes around the zoo a few times,
it is a moving, rolling, locomotive tribute
to the promise of safety at the end of the line.
It's why we stay such loyal passengers.

But should the train fall off the track, well,
we have exceptional navigational skills.
We brought the best mix tapes for the journey.
I was hoping you liked the Decemberists.
I was hoping you were all ukulele and drum brushes.
I was waiting to invite you to my porch swing.
Waiting for fancy lemonades and blender drinks.
Waiting for water before bedtime.
But the wait is nearly over.
This clunky old bus will pull up soon
because it is reliable. It's not always on time
but it will be here at its own damn pace.
We are fixtures at this bus stop.
The loyal passengers.
The not-drivers.
We take longer to get there.
It is always worth it.

TMNT, or When Did Turtle Power Become So Relatable

I am a teenage mutant ninja turtle;
a teenager in dog years and this year
I am dog tired. Sober seven years
But some days it feels like forty-nine.

I used to be super *cowabunga* fun, but I have changed.
I am the very dictionary definition of sober:

Serious. Moderate. Subdued.

I have mutated into someone less human. More of a shadow.
I could silently walk away and none would be the wiser.

I think I'm supposed to be a hero—?
—but this thin mask isn't fooling anyone.
We all know who I am. What I am.
In this version, Darkness is my uniform now.
Sobriety, a shell that I retreat into.

I am a mutation. I continue to change.
Not always for the better—
but I cannot live on pizza alone anymore.
It's evolve or die and I live on.

These evolutions may not be pretty.
I may not be your favorite anymore.
I wasn't better back in the day, just different—
but staying underground is how I was raised.

Every few years I think maybe it's time for a revival
but now fading into the background has become my best skill.
My weapon of choice.

I am a teenage mutant ninja turtle.
Tell me how silly I am. How much cooler I was
last century. I understand.
Call me fluke or freak or lucky break—
but I had a good run, didn't I? Made you smile?
made you feel safe and beautiful?
Isn't that why happy accidents like me
were created?

FSTB!

First grade, Fire Safety Week. We make construction paper fire trucks. Mine rules. I know this. I am the Picasso Pollock Van Gogh of wheels and ladders. My fire truck so good it is written by Stan Lee, inked by Jack Kirby. It is a goddamn collectors' item. Prizes given out. Someone must have misplaced mine. Teacher must have been drunk, must have been blind. Teacher needs art appreciation. Needs to take genius classes. Bell rings, we line up, busses line up. Bus doors open, we start to board. Stacy stands in front of me. Stacy drops something from her bag. Smokey The Bear. Plastic mascot, fire prevention hero, movable arms. Same size as Mego Spider-Man. Smokey winks at me, smiles. I shout to Stacy, *GOOD GOD WOMAN YOU ARE DROPPING WOODLAND CREATURES FROM YOUR SATCHEL, TAKE BACK THIS SEDUCTIVE URSINE REPLICA, ITS STEELY GAZE IS CORRUPTING ME*, but no answer. No reply at all, Smokey The Bear grips my hand, whispers *you're with me now*, ushers me onto the bus.

Smokey makes himself at home. Smokey and Mego Spider-Man become fast friends. Smokey teaches the Micronauts three new languages. Teaches my teddy bear judo and sees him through the 12-step program, gives my teddy bear his 24-hour sober chip. I ask, *shouldn't you go back to the little girl who misplaced you, who was so proud of your bravery that she made you the belle of show and tell?* Smokey exhales, throws his cigarette on a pile of dry twigs, stomps it out. Smokey leans in, says, *If I don't show, you won't tell*. Sings me James Taylor, "Fire and Rain," until I fall asleep.

Next night, school open house, parents and I in classroom surrounded by subpar fire engine art, some with cheap vinyl ribbons. Smokey told me to alibi, to stretch truth, to say I WON THIS BEAR AT SCHOOL. Parents beam at art critic reject teacher, thank teacher for plastic bear fire prevention prize. This, in slow motion, me realizing, *this is the thing they call lying*. This is what the bear put me up to. I have bitten the apple that the stupid cheap plastic bear gave me, swearing to me that it would taste like Fruit Loops, that I would eat it and be able to understand advanced trigonometry. Instead, I turn apple red. My tongue is a wildfire. My garden is burning down. Smokey The Bear tells me, *only you could have prevented this forest fire*.

Smokey The Bear is an asshole.

Blockhead

Well! Here comes ol' Charlie Brown!
Good ol' Charlie Brown...yessir!
Good ol' Charlie Brown...
How I hate him!

— Shermy, from the first *Peanuts* strip, October 2, 1950.

In second grade, you have go to school
dressed as an American hero,
so you dress up as Charlie Brown.
This is how it starts.

You leap in heart-first to everything after that.
You can either be called an optimist or a romantic
or you may be told you never learn.

You keep running at that football with the silly faith
that it won't be snatched away at the zero hour.

You accept this as fact and put it
in a panel with the word *sigh*
trapped in your throat bubble.

You stare across the classroom at the little red-haired girl,
knowing full well how this ends.
It's a bad holiday special at best.

You walk around off-balance
because your head feels too heavy
for your body to hold.

You grasp for five cent advice,
keep playing for a losing team—
for Halloween, you got a rock.

So you feel like a blah.
You think the only thing good is your grief;
but you know the story's not over.

You're the type who can make popcorn, toast, and jellybeans
and declare it to be a feast.

There are always new kites to fly,
regardless of how certain trees may try to spoil this.
You're not going to let rain take you off the pitcher's mound.
Your happiness is a warm puppy.
Used valentines are just fine.

Know that underneath that big blockhead,
you silly round-headed kid,
Chuck—you're a good man.

Comic Book Me

If you were to draw me in a comic book,
I would have a collar around my neck
and the leash attached would be held by my heart.

It'd be a cartoony heart, more like a valentine
and less like a fist. It would wear dark glasses,
not because it was blind, but because it was
sensitive. It would lead the comic book version of me
headfirst into many wacky adventures.

Funny ol' Comic Book Me, grabbing a big gooey ball of caution,
determining which way the wind is blowing,
and then throwing that caution directly into its breezy path—

Sometimes it splatters back into their brave face.

But Comic Book Me would wipe that goop
off of his thick black glasses
and wear the rest down his cheeks like war paint,
like he was the Ultimate Warrior of Love.

Somedays CBM has so much saccharine
in his delicate platelets
that Care Bears develop diabetes in his presence.

He goes in for a routine physical
and the x-ray reveals
a sap factory in his guts.
A library in his lungs.
Arrested development in his cynicism gland.

I sketch Comic Book Me onto napkins
and cash register paper. He seems
so small, so pure. He is a blob of a man,
all glasses and ears and unfading smiles.

As I fall asleep, I turn down the word balloons
emanating from the television box,
make sure all the borders of my panels
are tucked in, and I begin to inventory
all these sheep trying to get over this thought bubble fence.

Their soft bleats rise and fall
as I dream of a world
where Comic Book Me finds his muse,
who sings to him of a hopeful man
constructed out of creaky flesh and deep sighs.

Comic Book Me pledges to help this
seems-nice-enough fella find his purpose.
There will be, he vows to his cartoon heart,
the happiest of endings! It is a story
that I can invest in and believe

as I wait anxiously for the next issue.

Scream On

It was the 90's / and we'd spent the decade previous getting hacked / as in machete hacked / and slashed / as in straight razor slashed / we were 80's babies / raised on sequels / where the horrors were men / who were not men / demons born of man / occupying woods / camps / cabins / boiler rooms / living rooms / *chh chh chh* / *ahh ahh ahh* / single note piano songs became warning anthems / we had sex and we died / we drank and we died / we smoked pot and we died / but somewhere in the middle of this frenzy / we became punchlines / death puns / we multiplied / like sequels / became formulas / rehashes /retreads / and it became time / to breathe new life / into our fears / so we deconstructed / made our fear into jokes / told our friends / how to survive through the night / we slathered on soundtracks / cast ourselves to look like our favorite teen stars / like that might help us live longer / but not really / we still ran upstairs / had unprotected sex to sarah mclachlan tunes / shotgunned beers / answered the phone / opened the door / patted ourselves on the back for making it / all the while knowing / that which does not kill us / will probably do so in the sequel

Gardener
after a prompt by Nicole Homer

I buried my Jesus Liver in the backyard
      where I had previously
           watered the ground

with spilled wine or water
    or all the shitty beer
that was damn near water anyway
or
    full bladder
on hazy stumble nights

      in the center of the yard
         red flag planted over it
      like a grave (1990-2014)

The next morning,
grapevines hugging my house,
    fruit ripe and lush,

a field of wheat and hops
    whispering harvest songs

patches of potatoes
    from my vodka years

mighty oak buckets of malt
and barley
    ready for grist

and me, feeling   lighter
    almost ethereal

gathering
plucking
reaping

knowing that this magic
    this dreamy do-over magic

was by my own hand
    these wild oats sown
I called it my Jesus Liver
not because of the miracles
in the backyard

but because before this
    I had denied it three times

I am not religious
    but I am praying
it does not
    rise again

Todd Packer Is Committed to Being a Trash Human

and the rest of the office just wants him to go elsewhere.

Todd Packer was an internet troll
before any of you virgin nerds had an AOL account.

Todd Packer is Kentucky Deluxe in a Coke can.
He is the underbelly of Spring Break in Tallahassee.
Todd Packer thinks consent is kind of hot
but dancing around it is even hotter.

Todd Packer slings jokes about the gays, the women, the fat people.
Never mind that Todd Packer is not hot by most drink limits.
Never mind that Todd Packer slipped drugs into his apology cupcakes.
He is the devil on Michael Scott's shoulder; he is poking a hole into
the bottom of the popcorn tub.

Todd Packer's license plate reads "WL HUNG".

If doing The Scarn is gay, Todd Packer says to the camera,
then he is *the biggest queer on earth* with implied guffaws.

Todd Packer's homophobia is almost as pronounced as his misogyny,
which is no mean feat.
Todd Packer thinks his own daughter can be a bitch
just like her mother.
He is 1000 hotel rooms, a lot of interstates, a few hundred local bars.
There is no excuse for Todd Packer.
No origin story for the man who shit in Michael's office.

Todd Packer smokes menthols on the road.
Well liquor does the job just fine for Todd Packer.

The Pack-man dresses as a pregnant nun and wonders why you nerds
aren't laughing.

The Packster knows the second hour of a sexual harassment seminar
like the back of his hand.

Insert joke about genitals here.
Insert joke about sexuality here.
That's what she said.

Packer gets no redemption arc. Just gets fired in Florida
playing the part of a sexual predator all too well,
forever bouncing back like a horror movie villain
or a cameo role threatening to become a series regular.

not a robot / not a girl
after The Good Place

janet has a posse janet has a band
they're called

not a robot/
not a girl

and they're taking the void back they will rock all the puppies
all the puppies in the void will be created

and then rocked by all the janets

janet's band doesn't rock
in a straight line

not a robot/
not a girl

rocks in the loopy infinite cursive of time
they rock in the jeremy bearimy of it all
sometimes they rock on tuesdays sometimes at 2 AM
sometimes never

but there they all are a polyphonic spree of janets
good janet on lead vocals
bad janet on bass
disco janet funking the void on drums

all chanting to the beat

not a robot / not a girl
not a robot / not a girl

think of how many times in the jearimy bearimy was janet called

a robot
a girl

802 reboots
350 years of

oh girl robot! hey robot girl!

not a robot / not a girl

is playing throughout the universe
piped into the judges' chambers and the accountants' office—

not a robot / not a girl

goes great with the corner piece of cake—

jason says *janet, for a robot you're a great girl friend.*
janet says *i'm one of those three things*

not a robot / not a girl
was once called "the janets"
but they kept getting labelled as a girl group

not a girl not a magical slave robot
not a front desk lady—

it's got to be frustrating being misgendered
and dehumanized for all eternity;
seen as a broken punchline ready for reboot

it's almost funny
or not

What I Said to the Mirror

You stupid warrior.
You clutch the rose on your lapel too nervously.
You proud ill-attended bullfight,
sober and scraped out, needing
a reason to perform your *estocada*,
you have become a slow porch song.

These are the days when help is a four-letter word.
You, a voracious reader of your own riot act;
put the heavy book down. Please.
Take some delicate lessons.
The circus freaks look at you and sigh jealously
at the way you lance and retreat.
Hop in your time machine and travel to payday.
Buy yourself some fancy ale and a pocketknife.
Be the classiest hobo on the freight car.
Love the way your stubble feels.

Oh,
and you owe me twenty bucks.
So get famous soon.

This Was Supposed to Be a Buffy Poem

An HBO Special Presentation.
The year is 2010.
Carrie Fisher monologues about her addiction to booze and painkillers.
 In 2010 I am drinking my way across America on my first book tour,
wearing a "Do or do not, there is no try" t-shirt.
Carrie and me? Practically twins.

The write-ups for her one-woman show
call it "intoxicating." *Intoxicating* is a clever way
to describe a show about recovery. It's cute,
at least as adorable as all the times I performed on stages half-in-the-bag.

Spoiler alert: This was going to be a poem about Buffy Season Six
when Willow becomes addicted to magic
and Tara leaves her

Throughout her one-woman show,
Carrie Fisher maps out the trail of her failed relationships.
Some are celebrated in song; others become extended punchline.
My emotional Wikipedia states that song and punchline are my two favorite coping mechanisms,
not counting the abracadabra of another round.

Once you get a taste of the magic,
you do not want to put it down.
Makes you burn brighter. Willow knew.

The bodies left in its wake, good people consumed fast and tossed aside
like empty bottles, they know.

Ask any LA bar regular about their Andy Dick story.
Everyone in Los Angeles has one---
it's become almost mythic:
the levels of his inebriation, his insane behavior.

During my Andy Dick story,
Andy gets mad and yells at me,
WHERE'S *YOUR* SHOW, MISTER?
WHERE'S YOUR SHOW?
to point out that my magic is not as powerful as his.
My magic is a mere card trick. A paper flower tucked in a sleeve
and in this moment, I feel so very small.

As if millions of voices suddenly cried out in terror and were suddenly silenced.

But this is not about me. It was supposed to be about Willow.
Or Carrie.
Or Los Angeles.
Or magic.

Buffy closes the Hellmouth on May 20, 2003.
It takes eleven more years for me to kill my own demons.
Two years later, one of my recovery heroes
drowns in moonlight, strangled by her own bra.

 am still here, though, learning how to make magic,
through wishes or prayers or sleight of hand.
I am a one-man show, soaked in song and punchline,

trying so hard not to be cancelled;
trying hard not to go up in smoke.

---

1 Carrie Fisher, when speaking of George Lucas' rule that there was no underwear in space or Star Wars, reported "that no matter how I go, I want it reported that I drowned in moonlight, strangled by my own bra."

Oh My Stars

I think my relationship with astrology
is like being a casual fan of Marvel movies—

I don't know all the storyline details,
but it's easy enough to jump in,
I know some of the key players,
and I have a good read of what's going on.

Stars and moons, right?
Guiding you like a really sagacious box of Lucky Charms?
Yellow moons? Blue stars?
Helping you steer like Yoda riding shotgun?
Star maps? Not the Hollywood kind—but stars as maps?
I am starting to pay attention to these flirty cosmic blinks
and where they are pointing me.

It is my understanding
that with a Capricorn ascendant and Sagittarius moon,
I've got well-aimed, grounded earth energy.
No one warned me you were dressed in a small earthquake
and I would be shaking for weeks after.
Some called it a crater, I called it leaving quite the impression.

When you cascaded into my flight pattern—
celestial lightning rod that you are—
thrilling and spilling over with swords and wands and star stuff,
I recognized you as a constellation I immediately gravitated to.
And even though we were both a little broken and prone to veering off path,
doesn't that describe most shooting stars?

To say you turned on those beacons—the stars—for me is a bit much
You merely changed a few of their light bulbs,
tidied up the place, made sure I saw all the oranges and the blues
you worked so hard to polish.
It's a nice aesthetic. You did a stellar job.

Some days I wonder about what tarot cards were drawn
to allow two comets to travel on the same path
if even for just a tiny portion of the sky.
I wish I knew more about tarot.
I wish I knew more about comets.

I know there's a comet that shows up every 80 years
so you'd best appreciate it
if you're lucky enough to share its space.
Until then, I am a little starstruck
to simply have been in your orbit.
This is a comet tale for the ages.

Please do not hush me with the argument
that the stars burned out years ago,
that what we are looking at are ghosts and cover songs.
I am inviting the ghosts to all my usual haunts.
I love listening to the cover songs.
I am dancing under these stars
poorly but earnestly
like a nervous Midwestern boy--

a boy who makes mixtapes full of cover songs
for fiery technicolor meteorites
in hopes that they both can find their way home,
or at least help each other become a safe place to land.

Ghost at an Open Mic
after CJ Lance

She taps on the mic, whispers
is this thing on? Taps on her
chest. *Is this thing on?*

She is not afraid of dying in this room.

The host says, *don't go over time*
as if time still held sway for this apparition.
As if she wasn't the definition of timeless.

She is afraid that her metaphors
are see-through. Translucent.
That her word choice is not solid.

All we know is how ethereal she sounds.
How these words will cling to us
and leave an indelible mark.

I feel so at home here, she says.
and thanks us, as if we didn't gather
hoping she would be here;
hoping we would be so gently
haunted.

Now That I Have Your Attention

Hey. Hey.

I had a dream about you. The one where you were a ninja
and I was a chameleon.
The one where you were just kicking it
and I was just blending in.
The dream where we forgot what gender we were
and laid eggs in our prom dresses and hypercolor tuxedos,
giving birth to penguins and butterflies.
Hey.

I had a vision of you. All one with the forest,
wearing a moss hoodie, calling all the trees O.G.
and singing the woodland version of "Single Ladies":
if you like it, put another tree ring on it.

Hey. Hey there.

I promise I haven't dissolved any squares of paper
on my errant tongue; I haven't sipped any tea
made from frog parts or ingested mind medicine.
It's just sometimes you make me step
outside the box. The box attached to a piece of tin foil
and dandelion vines. You make me see things
the way they should be seen.
So *hey.*

I think it's time we saddled up the chihuahuas
and boogied our sweet behinds over to
Virgin Margaritaville. I hear they've got unlimited
hot wings and it's so sick that the boogie fever
gets contracted there three times a day.
Hey. Is for horses.
So saddle up and let's get hot to trot. Let's get so completely
conscious.
Hey. This love is a marathon, never a sprint.
Take your time. I'll be the homeboy
where the heart is. Dreaming just over
the speed limit. And this rollercoaster seats two.
And when I mean to say,
my goodness you're the best opus God ever put to my ears

or *how in the Nine Realms did you ever get to be
so damned right here, right now*

or *thank you for your clumsy grace and your belief
that all things fallible make the best lessons*

I become the most nervous out of all the nellies.
My teeth get so small; my tongue, a struggling fish,
and my lips clock overtime from beatboxing your praises.

I mean all this and more but I can't picture a thousand words
worthy of how my heart works when you wind it up.

I am reduced to single syllables. Like

Oh.

My.

And *Hey*

Lay Me Down
after "Acceptance Speech" by Mindy Nettifee

Now I lay me down
          really really down.
Now I lay me clinically down
with reruns of *Criminal Minds*
whispering from the TV at Volume 5,
          really really down.

Now I lay me down but do not fall asleep
for this brain is paved with half-sketched plans
on a slate I can never seem to wipe completely clean—

Now I lay Now I am down. Now I lay down in pastures
that are greener over on that side. The grass is wet
but I am dry. I am a dusty road between California and Oklahoma,
I am blessed to have been rest stop and oasis before I flooded.

This prayer is for the recovery I have made
in the recovery I swim through. Praise be this arid lake.
Praise be the same five musicals I sing as I row across it.
Praise be to *Les Miserables* allowing me to sing revolution in my
cubicle.

Thanks be for Scranton and Pawnee,
for Stars Hollow and for Sunnydale.
Hands in the air for the Multiverse and the MCU.
Praise be imaginary homes away from home.

Thank you for everything I am not in the face of everything I am.

Praise be the extra 45 pounds
Praise be the blotchy skin
the ulcer, the antacids, the constant negotiation
with this body.
Thanks for the autumnal coating turning to winter.
The uneven beard, the silver streaks, the eyebrows that grow
   like old-timey weeds or deeply European grandfathers.
The white forests in the ears.

Huzzah for the bifocals that slide down the bumpy ski slope
of a nose!
Turn it up for the diminishing hearing!
        (No, please--turn it up—and put-on captions)

To the songbird in my throat that clocks in when he feels like it--
   lift every voice and jam the fuck out! *Amateur* is French for lover!

Give it up for the strange fire that is this depression.
        Is it the Eternal Flame that the Bangles crooned about?
Is it the light that will never go out?
What a gift; being able to soundtrack our hearts!
Three cheers for the hopeful ways we mistake endorphins for love!
Four cheers for therapy that will not let me sit in the Self-Flagellating
Section anymore!

Praise be for the anxiety that feels like a thousand hot needles
as I wait for the bus, as I wait to cross the street.
Praise for the stress ball in my pocket,
the Vitamin C lozenge in my pocket,
the spare change in my pocket,
the lint in my pocket.

Praise for paychecks that shrink when exposed to daylight—
for the lenders with criminal rates
Praise be robbing Peter,
praise be paying Paul a 300 percent mark-up.

Yes to rice. Yes to beans. Yes to corn tortillas.
Yes to stretching a dollar so far and so wide it is almost transparent.

Hallelujah, I am broken.
Hallelujah, my friends keep me glued together.
Glory be, all I want is medicine and magic.
All I want is for this weight to lift from my body.
From my kept and taken soul.

All I want is to stay ridiculous with gratitude.
Praise be, I am grateful. Praise be, I am ridiculous.
Glory be, all I want is to rest.

Now I lay me really truly down.
But that doesn't mean
that I won't accept help getting back up.

Tuesday Night at the Sober Bar

one of the regulars
sits cross-legged on the barstool
and demands

ANOTHER SHOT!
OF WHEATGRASS!
AND A MANGO SMOOTHIE, PLEASE,
THIS TASTES LIKE A LAWNMOWER!

Tuesday Night at the Sober Bar
men sit without swaying,
using lines like
I am so hydrated right now.

The impulse control is off the charts.
Everyone here knows exactly
what they're doing.
The late-night texts composed in this place:
all super deliberate.

We've installed a ramp straight to the doorway
because we know twelve steps don't work for everybody.
Make your way in at your own pace.
The revolving door's always open.

There's a dude slumped over in a booth trying to kick
caffeine. He's very quick to anger
but too slow to properly swing at ya.

We have a drink special, pineapple juice and club soda,
called The Apology.
It gets asked for left and right.
There are SO many Apologies in a sober room.

Are there meetings here? Of course!
The Advanced D&D group meets every Sunday!
They're currently playing the Pink Cloud campaign,
Wherein our heroes have limited immunity!
Or at least it feels like they do!
It's a beginner's campaign!

Speaking of games:
Thursday at the Sober Bar, it's Trivia Night,
with questions like
FOR 10 POINTS: WHAT HAVE YOU DONE IN THE PAST 20 YEARS?
FOR 20 POINTS: WHAT could YOU HAVE DONE?
FOR 50 POINTS: WHAT IS AN ADDICT?
FOR 300 POINTS: WHY SHOULD WE BELIEVE YOU'VE CHANGED?
Fun for the whole family!
A game that everybody wins!

I promise, friends, The Sober Bar is not
a sad place. It is often sharp
and extra witty and the tip jar
is stuffed with five-dollar bills and smartass quips
like **HERE'S A TIP: TRY USING LICORICE ROOT
IF YA WANNA QUIT SMOKING!
ANOTHER TIP: DON'T TRY TO SMOKE IT**

Last call at the Sober Bar
and the jukebox has gone from
Recovery to Hang Me Up to Dry.
It's rattled off anthems and diversions
It's raised a glass to freedom
And for its last number
it plays a little small change as last call anthem
to get the patrons back to their binging
        binging Netflix
                binging *One Day at A Time*
                          (of course)

Lights Up. Tabs closed.
Stragglers singing to the night air:

The piano has been drinking
Not me
Not me
Not me
Not me
Not me.

Benediction for the Church of Common Sense

Go forth and skip stones
but not for sport or points.
Skip them in a non-competitive fashion,
like you are sending them on a speedboat to Mermaid Island.

This is your body, given to you.
Get a massage.
Sit under a tree and picnic your ass off.
Find your feel-good places and give a tour
to those who will not leave their trash lying around.
Show them to yourself.
You are a labyrinth;
role-play as yourself and discover all your treasure.

Dancing is optional. Head-nodding is healthy.
Tapping your fingers on the desk is drum heaven.
Make this your office karaoke jam. Solos are encouraged.
Go forth and watch movies where people kiss.
If you don't like kissing, replace *kiss* with *punch*.
If punching isn't your thing, replace *punch* with *laugh*.
If you don't approve of laughing, sit in the corner
and put on the Grumpasaurus outfit.
Go ahead.
We'll wait.

Praise be to chocolate.
Praise be to French fries.
Find the Holy Spirit in that bowl of cheese grits,
in that birthday card,
in that Pez dispenser.
Hell, that Pez dispenser fits twelve Holy Spirits. Share.

When two or more of you are gathered, bring board games.
Especially ones that make you blush.
Bring post-its and write down your favorite adjectives.
Act them out. Except maybe *lugrubious*,
which is more fun to say than to be.

Act like you know.
If you don't know, and you get caught,
blame it on the boogie.

I bid you warm towels.
I bid you good reception.
I bid you a perfect sandwich.

In the name of single moms, 7-11 employees, hat-wearing hedgehogs, superhero sidekicks, the high scorer on the Ms. Pac-Man machine at the bowling alley only known as ASS.

In the name of second chances, rides with the top down, toasted bagels, and Molly Ringwald circa *Pretty in Pink*.

In the name of non-ironic cover tunes, beverages with names like Razzleberry Mountain Blast, and cute little otter babies.

In the name of the gamblers, the jokers, the tiny dancers, the gypsies, the tramps, the thieves, the boxers, and any other profession that may have had a song dedicated to it on late '70's AM radio.

In the name of those who broke our heart, those who healed it, and people who hug with conviction.

Go forth and be spontaneous. Go forth and be sexy. Go forth and be Batman.

So it is. Let it be.

Let it be outstanding.

About the Author

Rob Sturma, when not doing some form of mild accounting, is a full-time nerd and the editor of *FreezeRay Poetry*, an online pop culture-themed literary journal established in 2014. His past editorial projects include zombie-themed poetry anthology *Aim For The Head* and superhero poetry anthology *MultiVerse*, both on Write Bloody Publishing. His own work has been featured in a number of keen anthologies including *Dark Ink, Working Stiff, Learn Then Burn 2,* and *Don't Blame the Ugly Mug*.

He lives in Oklahoma City, OK, where he helps curate the Red Dirt Poetry open mic, finds all the weirdest free streaming sites/apps, plays Super Nintendo, and stays forever in love with all things pro wrestling.

Acknowledgements

Thank you to the editors of the following publications where these poems previously appeared, sometimes in different forms:

"1984," "Sharp," "What I Said to the Mirror," and "Bedtime Story" were originally published in *Miles of Hallelujah*, Write Bloody Publishing, 2009.

"The Day Before Rock & Roll," "The Midnight Hour + The Art of Waiting," "Andre The Giant is Alive and Well and Working at the Circle K on 39th and Penn," "Stop Me if You've Heard This Before," and "Unsexy Beast" were previously published in altered form in *Why You Tread Water*, Tired Hearts Press, 2014.

"Popeye The Sailor Ruminates on Love" was previously published in *MultiVerse*, Write Bloody Publishing, 2014.

"Band Geek" and "Comic Book Me" were previously published in altered form in *Learn Then Burn 2: This Time It's Personal*, Write Bloody Publishing, 2014.

"Paul Heyman and I Go To Hot Topic Because It's BOGO T-Shirt Weekend" was originally published in *Drunk in a Midnight Choir, Volume 1: Welcome to the New Hallelujah*, DMC Press, 2015.

"Scream On" was originally published in Dark Ink: A Poetry Anthology Inspired by Horror, Moon Tide Press, 2018.

Thank You

Thanks to the Red Dirt Poetry fam who took me in immediately when I landed in Oklahoma and keep teaching me how community works every Wednesday.

Thanks to the *FreezeRay* staff for continuing to keep me open and ready for all the amazing voices that come through our inbox and for being tough on these nerds.

Thanks to Eric Morago for believing in me and my work for a hot minute now and for being a shining example of how to be a compassionate visionary.

Thanks to Kristen Grace for providing some serious editorial chops to a good portion of this manuscript, for the homespun stories and laughter as medicine, and for opening me up in a year full of closed doors. To say you've made me better is not hyperbole.

To everyone who helped keep me afloat with encouragement, love, and Real Talk when needed, in no particular order: Randy and Carolyn Sturma, Dawn and Brett Littlefield, Joe Hernandez-Kolski, Nicole Homer, Jack Tapestry, Sara Yoko, Victoria Bautista, Jean Alger, Mikkel Snyder, and all my imaginary friends on teevee, in the comics, and the movies. Onward, friends and family. I am grateful for you all.

Also Available from Moon Tide Press

Sh!t Men Say to Me: A Poetry Anthology in Response to Toxic Masculinity, (2021)
Flower Grand First, Gustavo Hernandez (2021)
Everything is Radiant Between the Hates, Rich Ferguson (2020)
When the Pain Starts: Poetry as Sequential Art, Alan Passman (2020)
This Place Could Be Haunted If I Didn't Believe in Love, Lincoln McElwee (2020)
Impossible Thirst, Kathryn de Lancellotti (2020)
Lullabies for End Times, Jennifer Bradpiece (2020)
Crabgrass World, Robin Axworthy (2020)
Contortionist Tongue, Dania Ayah Alkhouli (2020)
The only thing that makes sense is to grow, Scott Ferry (2020)
Dead Letter Box, Terri Niccum (2019)
Tea and Subtitles: Selected Poems 1999-2019, Michael Miller (2019)
At the Table of the Unknown, Alexandra Umlas (2019)
The Book of Rabbits, Vince Trimboli (2019)
Everything I Write Is a Love Song to the World, David McIntire (2019)
Letters to the Leader, HanaLena Fennel (2019)
Darwin's Garden, Lee Rossi (2019)
Dark Ink: A Poetry Anthology Inspired by Horror (2018)
Drop and Dazzle, Peggy Dobreer (2018)
Junkie Wife, Alexis Rhone Fancher (2018)
The Moon, My Lover, My Mother, & the Dog, Daniel McGinn (2018)
Lullaby of Teeth: An Anthology of Southern California Poetry (2017)
Angels in Seven, Michael Miller (2016)
A Likely Story, Robbi Nester (2014)
Embers on the Stairs, Ruth Bavetta (2014)
The Green of Sunset, John Brantingham (2013)
The Savagery of Bone, Timothy Matthew Perez (2013)
The Silence of Doorways, Sharon Venezio (2013)
Cosmos: An Anthology of Southern California Poetry (2012)
Straws and Shadows, Irena Praitis (2012)
In the Lake of Your Bones, Peggy Dobreer (2012)
I Was Building Up to Something, Susan Davis (2011)
Hopeless Cases, Michael Kramer (2011)
One World, Gail Newman (2011)
What We Ache For, Eric Morago (2010)
Now and Then, Lee Mallory (2009)
Pop Art: An Anthology of Southern California Poetry (2009)
In the Heaven of Never Before, Carine Topal (2008)

A Wild Region, Kate Buckley (2008)
Carving in Bone: An Anthology of Orange County Poetry (2007)
Kindness from a Dark God, Ben Trigg (2007)
A Thin Strand of Lights, Ricki Mandeville (2006)
Sleepyhead Assassins, Mindy Nettifee (2006)
Tide Pools: An Anthology of Orange County Poetry (2006)
Lost American Nights: Lyrics & Poems, Michael Ubaldini (2006)

Patrons

Moon Tide Press would like to thank the following people for their support in helping publish the finest poetry from the Southern California region. To sign up as a patron, visit www.moontidepress.com or send an email to publisher@moontidepress.com.

Anonymous
Robin Axworthy
Conner Brenner
Bill Cushing
Susan Davis
Peggy Dobreer
Dennis Gowans
Alexis Rhone Fancher
Hanalena Fennel
Half Off Books & Brad T. Cox
Donna Hilbert
Jim & Vicky Hoggatt
Michael Kramer
Ron Koertge & Bianca Richards
Ray & Christi Lacoste
Zachary & Tammy Locklin
Lincoln McElwee
David McIntire
José Enrique Medina
Michael Miller & Rachanee Srisavasdi
Michelle & Robert Miller
Ronny & Richard Morago
Terri Niccum
Andrew November
Jennifer Smith
Andrew Turner
Rex Wilder
Mariano Zaro

Made in the USA
Columbia, SC
21 May 2021